POLLUTION

INFO PICS

BY HARRIET BRUNDLE

BookLife
PUBLISHING

©2019
BookLife Publishing Ltd.
King's Lynn
Norfolk PE30 4LS

All rights reserved.
Printed in Malaysia.

A catalogue record for this
book is available from the
British Library.

ISBN: 978-1-78637-915-3

Written by:
Harriet Brundle

Edited by:
Emilie Dufresne

Designed by:
Danielle Rippengill

Image Credits

Cover and throughout – Eky Studio, Maria Starus, LenaDushkina, Supriya07, billedfab, Tartila. 4&5 – Beresnev, nnnnae, Boyko.Pictures. 6&7 – Dzm1try, Finevector. 8&9 – Amanita Silvicora. 12&13 – piscari, supirloko89, avh_vectors. 14&15 – Dzianis_Rakhuba, Bakhtiar Zein, Maquiladora, Visual Generation, HappyPictures, Orakunya, SquishyDoom. 16&17 – Beresnev, avian. 18&19 – Alexandr III, Faber14, Raura7, Tartila. 20&21 – Sentavio, Visual Generation, miniwide, Biscotto Design, ViGor Art. 22&23 – Shany Muchnik, Colorcocktail, K-Nick, Usagi-P. All images courtesy of Shutterstock.com. With thanks to Getty Images, Thinkstock Photo and iStockphoto.

CONTENTS

Words that look like <u>this</u> can be found in the glossary on page 24.

ALL ABOUT
POLLUTION

Pollution happens when materials, known as pollutants, are put into the <u>environment</u>.

These pollutants are harmful.

4

The Earth is becoming more polluted every day.

Some forms of pollutants help to cause <u>global warming</u>, which is very bad for our planet.

We can all help to lower the amount of pollution on Earth.

5

AIR POLLUTION

When a harmful material is added to the air, it is called an air pollutant.

Pollutants enter the air from lots of different places.

There are over 1 billion cars in the world. Many cars burn <u>fossil fuels</u> to give them power.

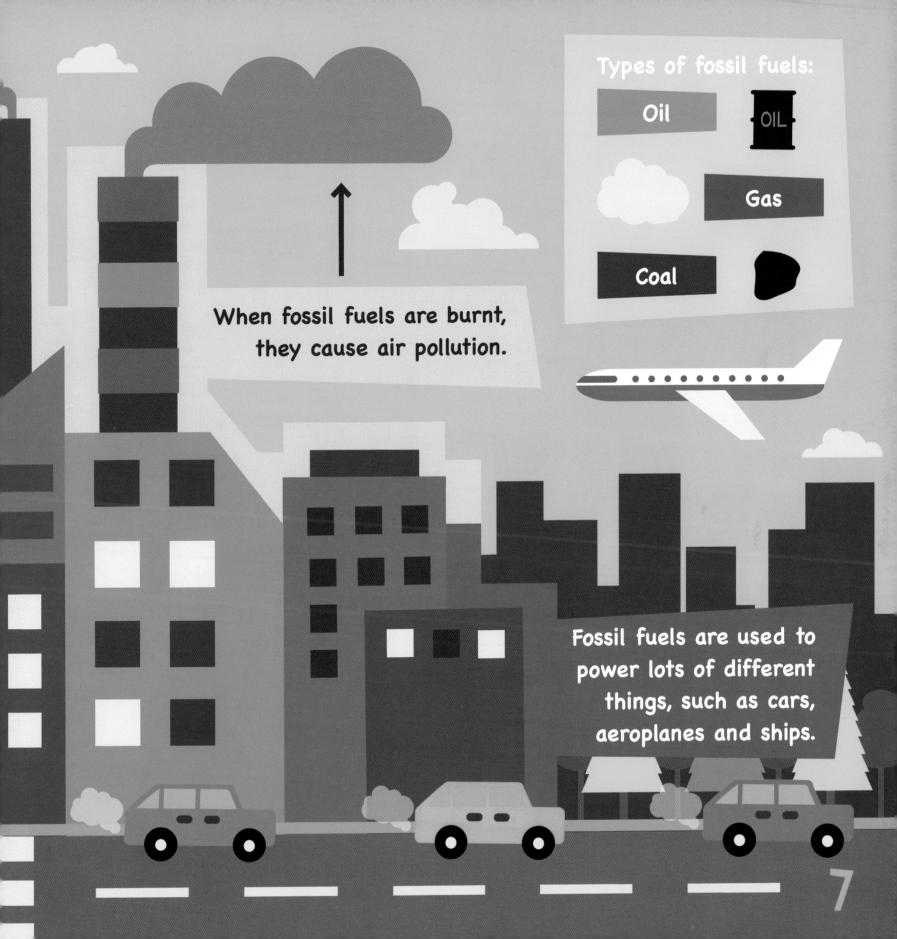

Types of fossil fuels:

Oil

OIL

Gas

Coal

When fossil fuels are burnt, they cause air pollution.

Fossil fuels are used to power lots of different things, such as cars, aeroplanes and ships.

7

Air pollution can cause sneezing, coughing, itchy eyes and more serious health problems.

Breathing in pollutants is bad for us. Millions of people around the world have had their health affected by air pollution.

Nine-tenths of the people on Earth live in a place with poor air <u>quality</u>.

A lot of air pollution is caused by humans, but it can also be caused by <u>natural</u> events, such as a volcano going off.

WATER POLLUTION

Water is polluted when harmful materials are added to it.

Around seven-tenths of Earth is covered by water.

Animals can mistake plastic floating in the ocean for food and eat it. This can cause them harm.

Turtle

Jellyfish →

Harmful pollutants can enter the world's water in many different ways.

HELP!

Ships leak oil into the ocean, which is harmful to plants and animals.

One of the ways pollutants are pumped into the ocean is through large pipes.

Ocean dumping is when pollutants are put straight into the ocean by humans on purpose. This could include rubbish or <u>sewage</u>.

LAND
POLLUTION

Every piece of rubbish you throw away must go somewhere.

Lots of rubbish ends up in <u>landfill</u> sites. These cause land pollution.

Pollutants from the rubbish in the landfill site leak into the nearby soil. This can harm plant and animal life.

It is thought that millions of tonnes of waste are put into landfill around the world every year.

Pollutants from landfill also leak into nearby water.

Here are some ways our land can become polluted.

When lots of trees are cut down, the soil where the trees used to be can become badly damaged.

Some farmers use harmful sprays on their crops to stop animals and insects from eating them. These sprays pollute the soil, the air and the nearby water.

16

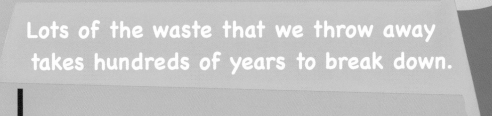

Lots of the waste that we throw away takes hundreds of years to break down.

Plastic bottles = around 450 years
Nappies = around 450 years
Plastic straws = around 200 years

LIGHT
POLLUTION

The over-use of human-made light causes light pollution.

Many night skies are brightly lit by human-made light when they should be dark. Light pollution is often worse in towns and cities.

Light pollution can be caused by things such as street lights, homes, stadiums, billboards and office buildings.

The **sky glow** from Los Angeles, in the US, can be seen from an aeroplane over 300 kilometres away.

Light pollution can make it difficult for some people to sleep.

Light pollution can confuse animals.

NOISE POLLUTION

Noise pollution happens when too much unwanted noise is being made, often for long periods of time.

Noise pollution can be harmful to humans and animals.

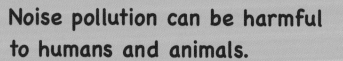

Noise pollution can come from construction, trains and aeroplanes.

Sounds above 85 decibels can harm your hearing.

A jet plane produces around 120–140 decibels and an electric drill produces around 95–100 decibels.

21

WHAT CAN WE DO?

Try to reduce how much rubbish you throw away.

Reuse items when you can. For example, take reusable bags to the shop instead of buying plastic ones.

Use energy-saving light bulbs.

NEV

PAPER

B

22

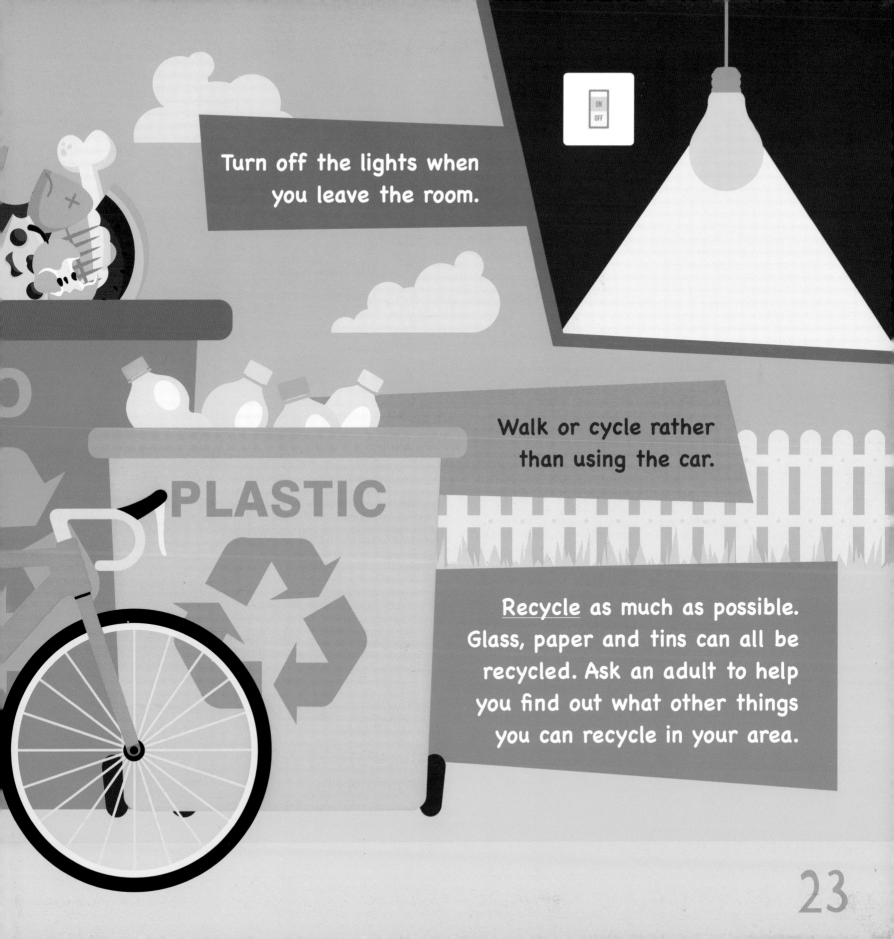

Turn off the lights when you leave the room.

PLASTIC

Walk or cycle rather than using the car.

Recycle as much as possible. Glass, paper and tins can all be recycled. Ask an adult to help you find out what other things you can recycle in your area.

23

GLOSSARY

construction	the act of building something
decibels	a way that sounds are measured
environment	the natural world
fossil fuels	fuels, such as coal, oil and gas, which formed millions of years ago from the remains of animals and plants
global warming	the slow rise of the Earth's temperature
landfill	where waste is buried
natural	found in nature and not made by people
quality	how good something is
recycle	use again to make something else
sewage	waste water from homes and factories that often includes human waste
sky glow	the brightness of the sky at night due to light pollution

INDEX